A Kid's Guide to Origami™

Making
ORIGAMI
SCIENCE
EXPERIMENTS
Step by Step

Michael G. LaFosse

The Rosen Publishing Group's
PowerKids Press™
New York

To my brother, David LaFosse

Published in 2004 by The Rosen Publishing Group, Inc.
29 East 21st Street, New York, NY 10010

First Edition

Editor: Jannell Khu
Book Design: Emily Muschinske
Layout Design: Kim Sonsky

Illustration Credits: Michael G. LaFosse
Photo Credits: All photographs by Adriana Skura

LaFosse, Michael G.
Making origami science experiments step by step / Michael G. LaFosse.
    v. cm. — (A kid's guide to origami)
Includes bibliographical references and index.
Contents: What is origami? — Table kite — Air foil — Water lily — Dish soap racing boat — Dart — Fan — Boat — Masu box.
ISBN 0-8239-6705-0 (library binding)
1. Origami—Juvenile literature. 2. Science—Experiments—Juvenile literature. [1. Origami. 2. Science—Experiments. 3. Experiments. 4. Paper work. 5. Handicraft.] I. Title. II. Series.
TT870 .L234227 2004
736'.982—dc21

2002153460

Manufactured in the United States of America

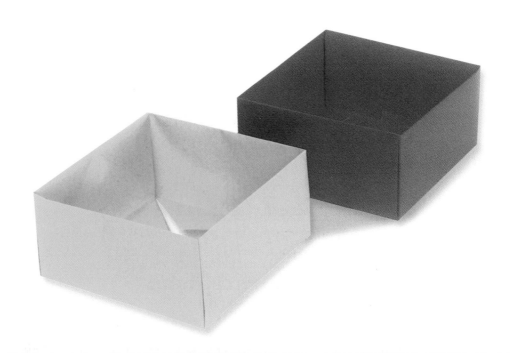

Contents

1 What Is Origami?   4
2 Table Kite   6
3 Air Foil   8
4 Water Lily Buds   10
5 Dish Soap Racing Boat   12
6 Dart   14
7 Fan   16
8 Boat   18
9 Masu Box   20
   Origami Key   22
   Glossary   23
   Index   24
   Web Sites   24

What Is Origami?

"Origami" means "paper folding." Most origami **projects** are folded from a single piece of paper and do not usually include any cutting. People of all ages create many useful and beautiful objects from folded paper, such as animals, flowers, airplanes, boats, boxes, hats, and toys.

Paper is easy to find and easy to work with. Many kinds of printer and gift-wrap papers work well for origami crafts. Origami directions use a special language of **symbols**, including dashed lines and arrows, to tell you how to fold the paper. The origami key at the back of this book on page 22 will show you what these symbols mean.

This book uses simple origami projects and scientific **experiments** to help you learn more about the world around you. The process of scientific discovery, called the scientific method, often begins with a question such as, "Which size paper will make a paper airplane fly the farthest?" To answer this question using the scientific method, we must come up with a **hypothesis**. A hypothesis is a guess or a suggestion that is made for the purpose of further study. Sometimes there are several possible hypotheses. To learn which is right, we can create experiments to prove or disprove each hypothesis. Feel free to write down new questions and possible answers whenever you think of them. Take a look at the origami key on page 22, then have fun doing these origami science experiments!

Table Kite

For this experiment we want to answer, "In what position will the Table Kite move across a table most **effectively**?" Make a guess as to what you think will happen and then conduct the following experiments. Place the kite open side down with one of the unfolded, diamond-shaped corners pointing toward you. Blow air across the top of the kite. Does the kite flatten down to the table? Why? Blowing on the top makes the air **pressure** on top greater than that under the kite, so the kite flattens. Next rotate, or turn, the kite so that one of the folded, triangle-shaped corners is pointing toward you. What happens when you blow air on it? When you turned the kite, some of the air that you blew traveled under the Table Kite, causing it to float just a little and move away from the force of your breath.

1

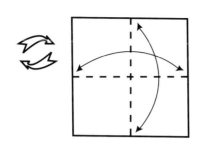

Use 8 ½-inch- (21.6-cm-) square paper. Valley fold the paper in half, edge to edge, each way. Unfold it after each fold. Rotate the paper so that it looks like a diamond.

2

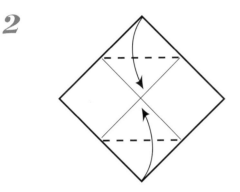

Valley fold two opposite corners to the center.

3

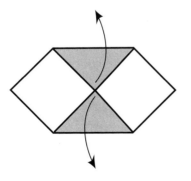

Unfold the paper.

4

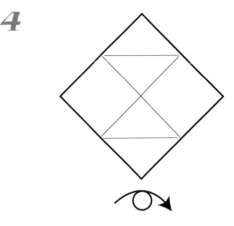

Turn the paper over.

5

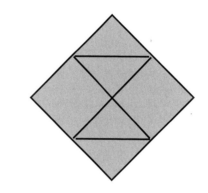

The finished Table Kite will look like this. There should be two triangle-shaped corners and two diamond-shaped corners. Try the experiments on the facing page. What happens if you use papers of different sizes? What if you turn the kite upside down?

Air Foil

For this experiment we want to find out, "Will paper of different shapes fall to the ground differently?" Take a sheet of paper and hold it at arm's length. Drop it. Notice how it falls to the ground. Take another paper and fold it over and over, to the middle of the sheet. Drop this paper in the same manner as the first paper. Did it fall more quickly than the flat, unfolded sheet? Air is full of gases and **particles** too small for us to see. However, you saw air's effect when you dropped the papers. This is called air **resistance**. The unfolded paper had more air resistance. The second paper had a smaller area. It was able to push through the air with less resistance, so it fell faster.

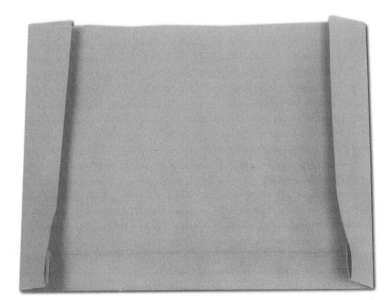

1

Use 8 ½-by-11-inch (21.6-x-28-cm) paper. Hold the paper out at arm's length and drop it. How does it fall?

2

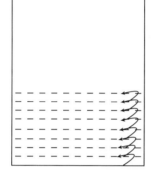

Valley fold the bottom edge of the paper, over and over, to the middle, to make a thick edge.

3

Hold the paper from the top, unfolded edge at arm's length and drop it. How does it fall? Does it fall faster than the unfolded sheet? Does it fall straighter?

4

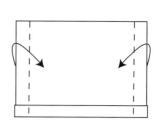

Valley fold the left and the right edges of the folded sheet. Let the folded edges stand up a little, to form fins. Hold the paper at arm's length and drop it. How does it fall?

5

Start with a new piece of paper. Fold as you did in steps 1 to 3 but fold more of the paper up, leaving only a little paper unfolded. Repeat the drop test. How does the paper fall? Faster? Straighter?

6

Valley fold fins at the left and the right edges. Repeat the drop test. Which paper falls fastest? Which will make the best flying wing? Try throwing each paper into the air in different ways, such as up, sideways, fast, and slow.

Water Lily Buds

For this experiment you will need two origami Water Lily Buds, and you will need a wet sponge, cloth, or paper towel. "What will happen to the Water Lily Buds if we wet them?" Place one of the buds on the wet sponge. Place the other on a dry surface. Does each open, like a **blossoming** flower? If so, which one opens faster? Paper is full of plant fibers that are hollow. Any material that has open spaces **absorbs** liquids. The paper buds on the wet sponge absorbed some of the water. As the paper absorbed water it **expanded**, making the folds of the bud open. Try this experiment with other materials such as wax paper, aluminum foil, and newspaper. What do you think will happen? Which materials are more absorbent?

1

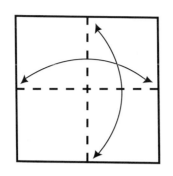

Use 8 ½ -inch- (21.6-cm-) square paper. Valley fold the paper in half, edge to edge, each way. Unfold it after each fold. Rotate the paper to look like a diamond.

2

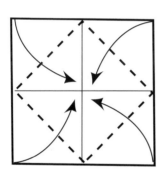

Valley fold all four corners to the center.

3

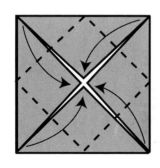

Valley fold all four new corners to the center.

4

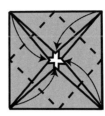

Valley fold all four new corners to the center.

5

This is the Water Lily Bud. Place it on a damp sponge and watch it blossom. How long does it take to open? Try it with other kinds and sizes of paper. Try it with wax paper. What happens? Why?

Dish Soap Racing Boat

For this experiment you will need a large bowl of water, a few drops of liquid soap, and a few Dish Soap Racing Boats folded from wax paper. Our question is, "What do we think will happen if we put a drop of soap on our boat?" Will it sink, float, or move in some direction? To understand this experiment, you first need to understand some of the **properties** of water. Still water has a layer of water **molecules** lined up to form a **surface tension**, or a kind of skin. Soap can destroy the structure of this skin, because the water molecules want to bond to the soap. Place a small drop of soap in the slit at the middle of the boat. What happens? The Racing Boat should suddenly race over the surface of the water. As the water pulls the soap out of the slit, it causes the boat to move in the opposite direction of the moving soap.

1

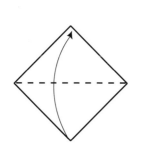

Use a piece of wax paper that is 8 ½ inches (21.6 cm) square. Position the paper so that it looks like a diamond. Fold in half, bottom corner to top corner. Unfold.

2

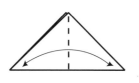

Valley fold in half, left corner to right corner, and unfold.

3

Valley fold the left and the right edges of the triangle to meet the middle at the crease.

4

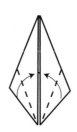

Valley fold the bottom left and the bottom right edges.

5

Unfold the two edges just a bit, to open the shape a little.

6

Add a drop of liquid soap here.

Float the boat in a large bowl of water. Using a toothpick or small stick, place a drop of liquid dish soap in the middle of the boat where the slit begins. The boat should suddenly move around as if powered by a motor. Try oil instead of soap. What happens?

Dart

For this experiment you will need one folded paper Dart. Notice that the folding method makes the nose heavy. Our questions are, "What makes our Dart fly straight and far? What **information** about this paper airplane and air pressure can I learn from how it flies?" What are your guesses? Throw the Dart to see how it flies. If it flew straight, then it was balanced for flight. The forward weight of the nose was equally balanced by the force of the air on the paper. If the plane's nose lifted as it flew, then the force of the air on top at the back of the plane was greater than the weight of the nose. If the nose tipped down, the force of the air on the underside at the back of the plane was greater than the weight of the nose. What happens when the plane lands? A paper airplane is supported by air while it is flying, but the force of **gravity** also pulls it toward the earth. The tail is supported more by the air, so the nose, or the heavy end, falls first.

1

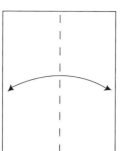

Use an 8 ½ -by-11-inch (21.6-x-28-cm) printer paper. Valley fold it in half, long edge to long edge. Unfold the paper.

2

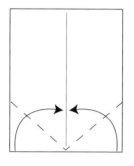

Carefully valley fold each half of the bottom edge to meet at the center crease line.

3

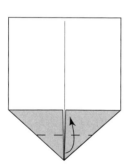

Valley fold up the nose point to meet the corners.

4

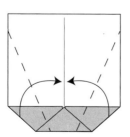

Carefully valley fold the two angled edges of the folded paper to meet at the center crease line.

5

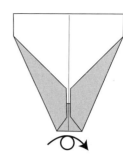

Turn the paper over.

6

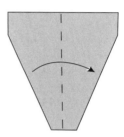

Valley fold it in half, wing to wing.

7

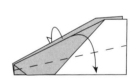

Valley fold the wing facing you, and mountain fold the other side. Carefully match the wing edges to the bottom edge of the Dart.

8

Back view of wings

Open out the two wings. Use this back view line drawing as a guide to the proper form.

Fan

This experiment requires several sheets of paper and some small, thin, light books. Our questions are, "How strong is unfolded paper versus folded paper? Why?" If you take a piece of paper and try to stand it on its edge, it quickly flops over. If you fan-fold a paper, you will see that the paper will stand because it is **rigid** and has a wider base. Fold two more of these Fans, using the same number of folds and the same kind of paper, and stand them up end to end to form a triangle. Place a small book across the tops

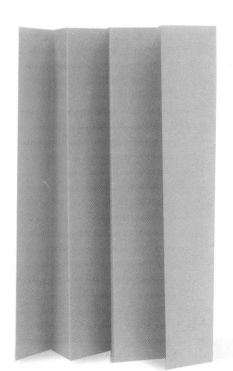

of the papers. Will the papers be strong enough to hold up the book? How many more books can you add before the paper posts cave in? How many more posts will you need to support another book? Would another folded shape be just as strong? Why or why not?

1

Use 8 ½ -by-11-inch (21.6-cm-by-28-cm) printer paper. Try to stand it on an edge. What happens?

2

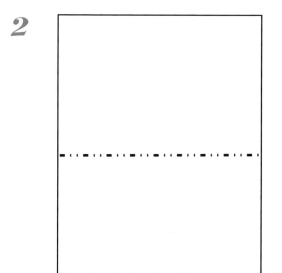

Mountain fold the paper in half and unfold it. Try the experiment. Does it work?

3

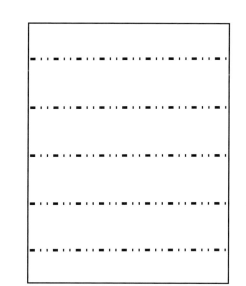

Mountain fold the paper as shown above.

4

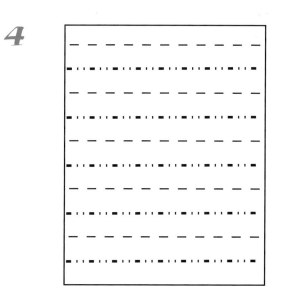

Mountain fold and valley fold an equal number of folds into the paper to make a fan. Now try your experiment with different numbers of fan folds. How strong is the fan with four folds, with eight folds, and with sixteen folds? Try folding the paper from the long end.

Boat

To do this experiment you will need several Boats folded from wax paper, and a pitcher that is full to the rim with water. Set the pitcher in a large bowl. The question we want to answer is whether objects of the same size have the same **mass**. What do you think? Let's experiment to find out. Place an object of equal size, such as a quarter, a bottle cap, or a small, flat pebble, in each Boat. To measure each object's mass, float the Boats one at a time in the pitcher. The mass of the object you are weighing **displaces** an equal mass of water. Measure the amount of water that comes out of the pitcher by dipping a 1-inch-wide (2.5-cm-wide) strip of paper towel into the water that spilled into the bowl. Hold each wetted strip next to the one before. What happened? You should discover that objects of the same size can have different masses.

1

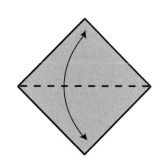

Use 10-inch- (25.4-cm-) square wax paper. Position the paper so that it looks like a diamond. Fold it in half, bottom corner to top corner. Unfold the paper.

2

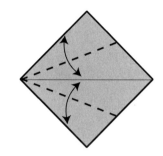

Valley fold the top and bottom left sides of the paper to meet at the crease. Unfold it.

3

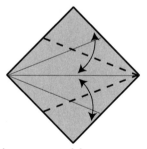

Valley fold the top and bottom right sides of the paper to meet at the crease. Unfold it.

4

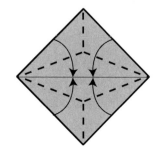

Valley fold the square's four edges to the center crease. The top and bottom corners will fold in half and rise in the middle. Flatten these corners to the right. Then fold them to the left.

5

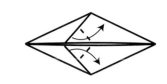

Valley fold each of the flattened corners over, one to the top corner and the other to the bottom corner.

6

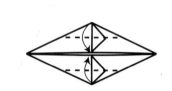

Flip over the two triangle shapes, left to right, and then flatten them.

7

Valley fold the top and bottom corners to meet at the center of the paper.

8

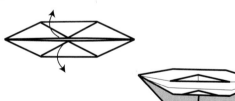

Open the paper in the middle and turn the paper inside out, forming the boat.

Masu Box

A *Masu* is a traditional Japanese wooden box used to measure beans, rice, and other grains. Our Masu Box will be made with paper. For this experiment you will need one sheet of paper and some objects, such as jelly beans, rice, or strips of paper. We want to figure out the **volume** of our Masu Box. If volume is the amount of space taken up by an object, how can we figure out the volume of the Masu Box? When we know a cube's length, width, and height, we can figure out its volume. What is our Masu Box's volume in jelly beans and rice? How many strips of paper does it take to fill up the box? What other **container** can you measure in this fashion? Have fun finding out!

1

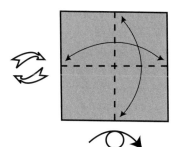

Use an 8 ½-inch- (21.6-cm-) square paper. Valley fold it in half, edge to edge, each way. Unfold it after each fold. Turn the paper over, and rotate it.

2

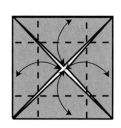

Valley fold all four corners to the center.

3

Valley fold each edge of the square to the center, then unfold the paper.

4

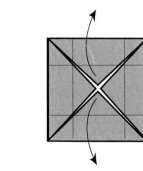

Open the top and the bottom corners.

5

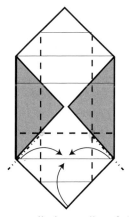

Make the box walls by valley folding up the left and the right sides and then the bottom edge. Use the creases to bring in the bottom corners. Look ahead at step 6 for the shape.

6

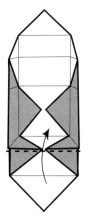

Valley fold the bottom corner. The paper point will go inside, to the bottom of the box.

7

Do step 6 on the top.

8

This is the finished Masu Box.

Origami Key

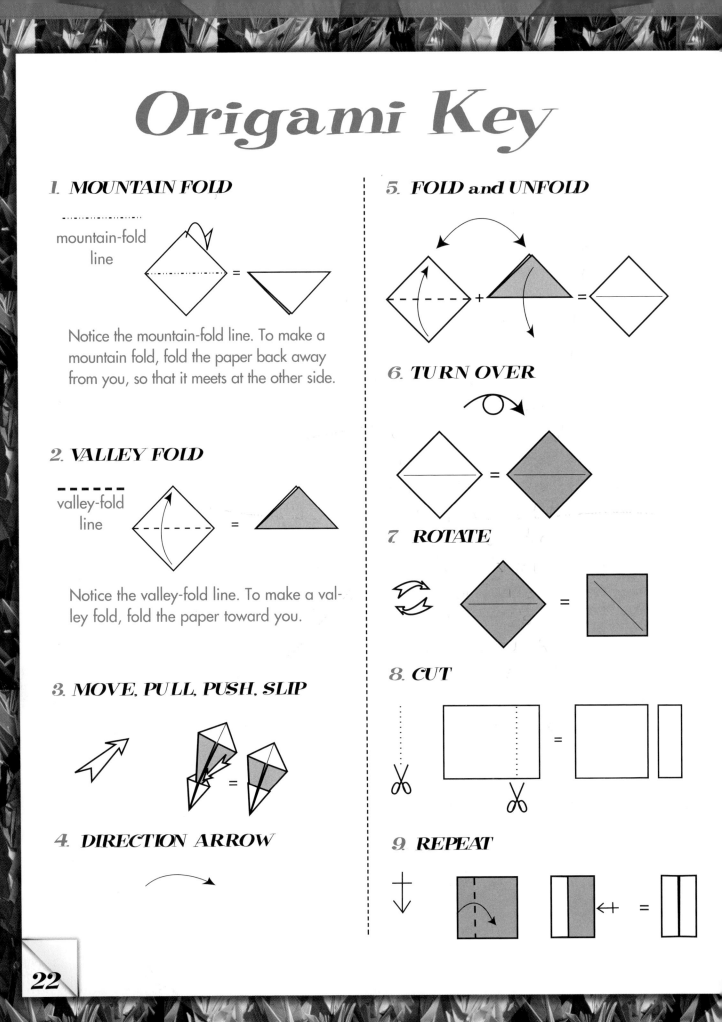

1. MOUNTAIN FOLD

mountain-fold
line

Notice the mountain-fold line. To make a mountain fold, fold the paper back away from you, so that it meets at the other side.

2. VALLEY FOLD

valley-fold
line

Notice the valley-fold line. To make a valley fold, fold the paper toward you.

3. MOVE, PULL, PUSH, SLIP

4. DIRECTION ARROW

5. FOLD and UNFOLD

6. TURN OVER

7. ROTATE

8. CUT

9. REPEAT

Glossary

absorbs (ub-ZORBZ) Takes in and holds on to something.

blossoming (BLAH-sum-ing) Flowering; producing fruit.

container (kun-TAY-ner) A box that holds things.

displaces (dis-PLAYS-ez) Moves out of position.

effectively (ih-FEK-tiv-lee) In a way that works.

expanded (ek-SPAND-ed) To have spread out, or to have grown larger.

experiments (ek-SPER-uh-ments) Tests done on something to learn more about it.

gravity (GRA-vih-tee) The natural force that causes objects to move toward the center of Earth.

hypothesis (hy-PAH-theh-sis) A possible answer to a problem.

information (in-fer-MAY-shun) Knowledge or facts.

mass (MAS) The amount of matter in something.

molecules (MAH-lih-kyoolz) The smallest bits of matter before they get broken down into their basic parts.

particles (PAR-tih-kulz) Small pieces of something.

pressure (PREH-shur) A force that pushes on something.

projects (PRAH-jekts) Special jobs that people do.

properties (PRAH-per-teez) Features that belong to something.

resistance (rih-ZIS-tens) A force that requires work to overcome.

rigid (RIH-jid) Stiff.

surface tension (SER-fis TEN-chun) The force that holds the surface of a liquid together.

symbols (SIM-bulz) Objects or pictures that stand for something else.

volume (VOL-yoom) The amount of space that matter takes up.

Index

A
airplane(s), 4, 14
air pressure, 6
air resistance, 8

B
boat(s), 4, 12, 18
book(s), 16
bowl, 18

F
fibers, 10
force, 6, 14

G
gravity, 14

H
hypothesis(es), 5

M
mass(es), 18
Masu Box, 20

P
paper towel, 10, 18
pitcher, 18

S
scientific method, 4
soap, 12
sponge, 10
surface tension, 12
symbols, 4

V
volume, 20

W
water, 10, 12, 18
water molecules, 12
wax paper, 10, 12, 18

Web Sites

Due to the changing nature of Internet links, PowerKids Press has developed an online list of Web sites related to the subject of this book. This site is updated regularly. Please use this link to access the list:
www.powerkidslinks.com/kgo/experime/